Glow-in-the-Dark Animals

LANTERN FISH

Sara Howell

PowerKiDS press.

New York

Published in 2015 by The Rosen Publishing Group, Inc.
29 East 21st Street, New York, NY 10010

First Edition

Editor: Katie Kawa
Book Design: Katelyn Londino

Photo Credits: Cover, p. 11 (lantern fish) Visuals Unlimited, Inc./David Wrobel/Visuals Unlimited/Getty Images; cover, pp. 1–24 (background texture) olesya k/Shutterstock.com; cover, pp. 10–11 (underwater backdrop), p. 18 Rich Carey/Shutterstock.com; p. 5, 13 Courtesy of NOAA; pp. 6–7 Richard Whitcombe/Shutterstock.com; p. 9 DR PAUL ZAHL/Photo Researchers/Getty Images; p. 12 U.S. Navy/Getty Images News/Getty Images; pp. 14–15 aquapix/Shutterstock.com; p. 14 (inset) http://commons.wikimedia.org/wiki/Krill#mediaviewer/File:Meganyctiphanes_norvegica.jpg; p. 17 Karen Doody/Stocktrek Images/Getty Images; p. 19 Solvin Zankl/© Nature Picture Library/Alamy; p. 21 Arthur Tilley/The Image Bank/Getty Images; p. 22 (coral) Andrea Izzotti/Shutterstock.com; p. 22 (lantern fish) http://upload.wikimedia.org/wikipedia/commons/c/c0/Lanternfish_larva.jpg.

Library of Congress Cataloging-in-Publication Data

Howell, Sara, author.
 Lantern fish / Sara Howell.
     pages cm. — (Glow-in-the-dark animals)
 Includes index.
 ISBN 978-1-4994-0148-6 (pbk.)
 ISBN 978-1-4994-0149-3 (6 pack)
 ISBN 978-1-4994-0147-9 (library binding)
 1. Lanternfishes—Juvenile literature. 2. Bioluminescence—Juvenile literature. 3. Adaptation (Biology)—Juvenile literature. I. Title.
 QL638.M9H69 2015
 597.61—dc23
                         2014026927

Manufactured in the United States of America

CPSIA Compliance Information: Batch #CW15PK: For Further Information contact Rosen Publishing, New York, New York at 1-800-237-9932

CONTENTS

LIFE AS A LANTERN FISH

Did you know that about 70 percent of our planet is covered by water? Most of this water can be found in Earth's oceans. In many places, the ocean is thousands of feet deep. Very little sunlight is able to reach below 656 feet (200 m).

Lantern fish are one kind of fish that can live in the deeper, darker parts of oceans. There are about 240 species, or kinds, of lantern fish. These small fish get their name from their ability to make light with their body. That ability certainly comes in handy in the dark ocean **depths**!

Lantern fish are one of the most common fish in the world's oceans.

NEWS FLASH!

Oceans are commonly split into areas called zones. The highest zone is called the sunlight zone. The middle zone is called the twilight zone because it gets only a little light. The deepest and darkest zone is called the midnight zone.

DOWN IN THE DEPTHS

Lantern fish live in oceans all around the world. Many stay in waters close to the coast near an area called the continental slope. This is the steep slope between the continental shelf and the deep, open ocean.

Lantern fish need to make their own light to survive in the deep, dark parts of the ocean.

Most lantern fish spend the daytime hours in deep waters up to 3,280 feet (1,500 m) below the ocean's surface. However, at night, they move closer to the surface. They stay just 30 to 330 feet (9 to 101 m) underwater after the sun sets.

NEWS FLASH!

The continental shelf is the area of a continent, or large mass of land, that goes into the ocean. The water there isn't as deep as it is in the open ocean.

A CLOSER LOOK

Lantern fish are small, thin fish. Some species can grow to about 12 inches (30 cm) long. Most are between 1 and 6 inches (2.5 and 15 cm) long, though. Species that live in deeper parts of the ocean are often brown or black. Others that live closer to the water's surface can be green, blue, or silver.

Most lantern fish have an **organ** called a gas bladder. The gas bladder helps the lantern fish stay at a certain depth without using a lot of energy.

Lantern fish are known for their large eyes and mouth.

NEWS FLASH!

A gas bladder is sometimes called a swim bladder. If a fish wants to go up, it fills the bladder with air. If it wants to go down, it lets air out of the bladder.

LIGHTS IN THE WATER

Lantern fish make light through a **chemical reaction** that takes place in their bodies. This is called bioluminescence (by-oh-loo-muh-NEH-suhns). The light that lantern fish produce can be either yellow, blue, or green. Different species glow in different colors. Males and females of the same species can also create different colors of light and flash their light at different speeds.

A lantern fish's light comes from special organs called photophores (FOH-tuh-fohrs). They're found in rows on a lantern fish's body and head. In many species of lantern fish, the photophores are near their tail fin or close to their eyes.

Scientists can tell one species of lantern fish from another by looking at the placement of photophores on the fish's body.

NEWS FLASH!

Lantern fish also commonly have photophores on their belly.

SCHOOLS AND SONAR

Lantern fish live in large groups, called schools. They use their flashes of light to **communicate** with each other and keep the school together. Different species of lantern fish often live at different ocean depths. Scientists believe this is so they don't have to **compete** with each other for food.

Schools of lantern fish are so large they're often detected by sonar. Sonar is a tool that uses underwater sound waves to find objects. The sound waves bounce off the large schools of lantern fish. In the past, this made scientists think schools of fish were the ocean floor!

Sonar is an important tool for scientists and navies around the world.

NEWS FLASH!

The **layer** of fish scientists once thought was the ocean floor is sometimes called the false bottom or deep-scattering layer.

ON THE MOVE FOR A MEAL

Scientists discovered the false bottom because the layer they thought was the ocean floor kept moving up and down. This happened because lantern fish move between deep and **shallow** waters to find food. Lantern fish are predators that follow their **prey** as it moves up and down in the depths of the ocean.

Zooplankton like this could be food for lantern fish!

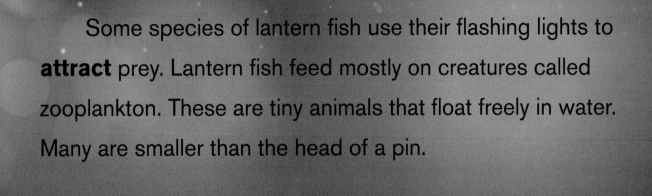

Some species of lantern fish use their flashing lights to **attract** prey. Lantern fish feed mostly on creatures called zooplankton. These are tiny animals that float freely in water. Many are smaller than the head of a pin.

NEWS FLASH!

Moving up and down, as lantern fish do in the ocean, is called moving vertically. The way lantern fish follow their prey from deep to shallow waters is called diel (DY-uhl) vertical migration.

AVOIDING PREDATORS

Lantern fish also move between deep and shallow waters to avoid predators. Lantern fish are an important part of many ocean food chains. They're food for whales, sharks, dolphins, and squid. They're also eaten by other fish, such as tuna, and birds, such as penguins.

Lantern fish's ability to produce light also helps **protect** them from predators. They're able to control the amount of light they produce to match the light around them. Predators then have trouble seeing the lantern fish. This is known as counterillumination.

Many animals that live in deep ocean waters, including the scaly dragonfish and some species of squid, use counterillumination to protect themselves, too.

NEWS FLASH!

Counterillumination helps
bioluminescent animals protect
themselves from predators
who hunt by looking up to
find prey above them.

LANTERN FISH BABIES

Because lantern fish's flashes of light differ between species and between males and females, it's likely they use their glowing ability to attract a **mate**. When it's time to **spawn**, a female lantern fish will **release** her eggs into the water. She can release between 100 and 2,000 eggs at a time.

Baby lantern fish, called larvae, are left to survive on their own after coming out of the eggs. Lantern fish have light organs from the time they're larvae. This means even baby lantern fish are bioluminescent!

Corals are other animals that spawn.
Like lantern fish, corals can glow in the dark!

NEWS FLASH!

Lantern fish larvae make up
nearly half of all fish larvae in
the world's oceans.

HEALTHY OCEANS, HEALTHY FISH

Lantern fish are some of the most common fish in the world's oceans. This doesn't mean they're safe from danger, though. Lantern fish often come into contact with pollution, such as garbage floating in the ocean. Scientists have found tiny bits of plastic in the stomachs of some lantern fish. This plastic is harmful to lantern fish as well as the animals that eat them.

Keeping oceans clean is an important way to keep lantern fish healthy. Healthy lantern fish play a part in keeping oceans healthy because they're part of so many ocean food chains.

People can help protect lantern fish by cleaning up garbage they find on the beach. This can stop plastic from getting into the ocean.

NEWS FLASH!

Scientists are still learning new things about lantern fish all the time. They study the times these fish use their ability to glow in order to find out more about how lantern fish communicate.

FUN LANTERN FISH FACTS

1 Lantern fish have large eyes to help them see more light in dark water.

2 One species of lantern fish doesn't have photophores and isn't able to produce light.

3 The chemical reaction that produces light in a lantern fish's photophores is the same reaction that makes a firefly glow.

4 Lantern fish produce cold light, which means they produce light without also producing heat.

5 Hector's lantern fish are caught by fisherman in waters off South Africa. They're used to make fish oil and fish meal, which is used to feed other animals.

6 Lantern fish make up about 65 percent of the fish in the deep sea.

GLOSSARY

attract: To cause to come close.

chemical reaction: The process by which matter is changed after coming into contact with other matter.

communicate: To share ideas and feelings.

compete: To strive for something that another person or thing is also striving for.

depths: Deep places in a body of water.

layer: One part of something lying over or under another.

mate: An animal that another animal makes babies with.

organ: A body part with a specific function or purpose.

prey: An animal hunted by other animals for food.

protect: To keep safe.

release: To let go.

shallow: Not deep.

spawn: The process by which male and female animals come together to lay eggs in water.

INDEX

WEBSITES

Due to the changing nature of Internet links, PowerKids Press has developed an online list of websites related to the subject of this book. This site is updated regularly. Please use this link to access the list: www.powerkidslinks.com/gitda/lanf